HEAVEN IS ON (

A NEW CREATION MYTH

BY
BONZAI HOLMES

MW00953233

ILLUSTRATED BY MADALYN FREEDMAN

I want to dedicate this book to the Oneness of Nature. For it is in living and observing that this book was inspired.

Special thanks to Naia Graham, my inspiration to know deeper love.

I want to thank Kaypacha Lescher, an astrologer, who has inspired me to look more deeply into the cosmos for all the signs... Thank you for reading the book.

I also want to acknowledge Madalyn Freedman, Illustrator of this book, for this would still just be rolling around in my head if she did not bring it to life with her brilliant artistry and vision.

And I also want to dedicate this book to my unborn child(ren) and to all the children of the world... who deserve to know and feel abundant love.

Here is a tale of Perspective,
one told through the eyes of the Collective.
Of Yang cruising through the Cosmos
in search of what he felt the most.
A longing to experience life in the flesh,
all the ways love weaves through the mesh.
Desire exhaled Creation,
and Light beamed a solar station.
One that spirals and twirls and pushes and pulls
the same way a carpenter uses his tools.
The elements are part of History,
and perhaps the greatest part of the mystery.
Of how it all works and exists,
a way to explain with a twist.
That birth is all about Biology,
and Earth was created from Astrology.
So as above, so below...
This is how the story goes...

With mighty Cardinal power,
Aries ascended upon the tower.
Not to say "I'm the best and you're the worst,"
but all to say "I come first."
It is passion that brought the asteroids together.
In one big bang, space dust came into collision.
It was then the Cosmos made a decision.
"I want you, with all my heart -
at least here we can make a start."

CARDINAL FIRE: ARIES

So with the energy of the sun,
a feminine presence had begun.
A planet felt holy desire,
and that is how Earth was born of fire.

FIXED EARTH: TAURUS

Earth clung to gravity and felt the cold of space.
It was in that love, she fixed herself into place.
With dense mass now, like a bull
she began to harden with the cool.
"I am here now" she says, Spirit formed to matter.
"Let's build existence, and let's do it together."

And so the dance began
and caused utter attraction.
For the laws state -
that for every action,
there is a reaction.

The fire needed to breathe
and the Earth needed to expand.
Magnetic force drew in more love
and the moon said "I'm your woman."
A mutable shifty occurrence, Polarity
held them close and gave each some space.
The Earth could see herself more,
by looking at the moon's face.
"You are my partner - that is no lie,
we are made One - by the Gem in I."

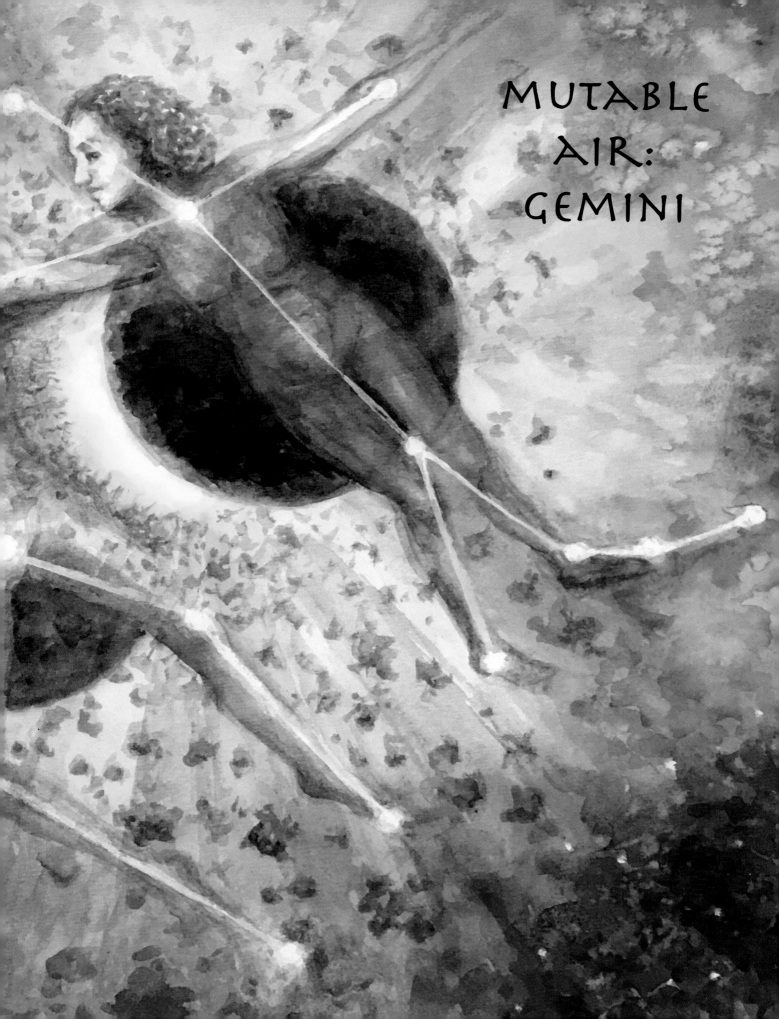

MUTABLE
AIR:
GEMINI

CARDINAL
WATER:
CANCER

The void began to weep and tears were the answer.
A planet wanting to grow so quick -
it needed to soothe its Cancer.
Relaxed and cooled now to keep from getting hotter,
the Oceans were created from Cardinal Water.

Fire then - fixed on pride -
erupted from the cool
and roared out, "I cannot hide!"
"I represent the sun
that I am in the image as,
it is from divine spirit
that Earth has her mass."
Pure Energy,
a place of synchronistic synergy.
"I am out of the cage -
The world is my stage."

FIXED FIRE: LEO

MUTABLE EARTH: VIRGO

Continents and plates started to form
Earth was feeling her grooves.
"I am the land you dreamed of,
all created from our moves."
"We are doing this together
every part of the task.
If we want to receive,
all we do is Ask."

The connection was electric, the union of Earth and sky.
Polarity gave them balance, and air began to fly.
"I am the Protector, let my presence be a shield.
I offer up expanse and provide a force field."

CARDINAL AIR: LIBRA

Earth felt the sky's compassion and frost fixed on the surface.
Even through bitter cold – Love still had a purpose.
The Oceans turned to ice with a frostbitten sting,
such deep emotion, the Planet longed for a ring.

FIXED
WATER:
SCORPIO

MUTABLE FIRE: SAGITTARIUS

A ring of fire that is,
to keep up the heat.
All of it was alchemy
a magical lucid dream.
A little bit here,
a little bit there,
the elements mixed around.
Paradise created
with many feels and flavors.
A place so good,
for all creatures to savor.

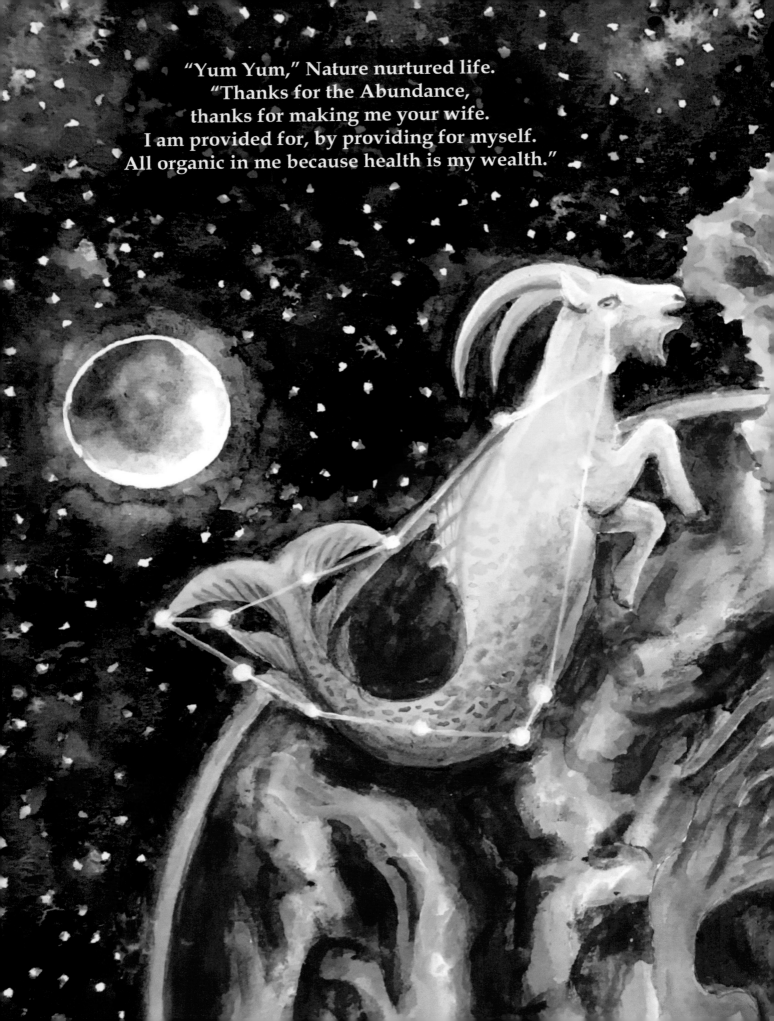

"Yum Yum," Nature nurtured life.
"Thanks for the Abundance,
thanks for making me your wife.
I am provided for, by providing for myself.
All organic in me because health is my wealth."

CARDINAL EARTH: CAPRICORN

"Got to keep up, there are many breeds.
Got to plan ahead, water every seed.
I need a bird's eye view to keep watch over the crowds
You know you see me when rain falls from the clouds."

MUTABLE
WATER:
PISCES

"My cup runs over, my roots feel it flow
Every nook and cranny - I learn to let more go."
To give and to take, to end and begin,
A flow of the Universe - a true teacher of Yin.
Evolution continues, sensitive fruition.
All this came about
by trusting intuition.

Trust Gaia to know - how to harmonize and adapt. Co-existing in Peace ,
A place that can be mapped. 2-leggeds, 4-leggeds, wing-ed ones and all,
knowing that we come from the same source, we do not need to sprawl.

We can spread out, though,
to feel our individual worth,
because what the Divine has made
is Heaven here on Earth.
A global village on a journey
through time and space
So give in to the love and magic
that birthed the human race.

About the Author

Eric Michael , a.k.a Bonzai Holmes, is a builder, farmer, and outdoor educator who has been inspired by the elements and astrology since early years of high school. Originally born and raised in Virginia, he has traveled a fair amount to lead him home on Hawai'i island, a perfect place to witness many faces of the planet in one small place. His mission in life is to support the planet in all ways sustainable... mainly through Permaculture design and overcoming problems with idea sharing and love. He resides on beautiful Kohala Mountain, in the Pacific Ocean.

About the Illustrator

Madalyn Freedman, illustrator of books for children, resides in Hilo, Hawai'i with one human and several animal friends. She has worked as a sailor, rigger, artist, and cook, among other things. Her current projects include studying at the local University and trying to live as sustainably as possible. You can check out her work at madalynillustrator.wordpress. com.

89967525R00020

Made in the USA
Middletown, DE
19 September 2018